JESUS GIRL
Doing Real Life!

JESUS GIRL
Doing Real Life!

From Stripper... To Preacher

ANDREA THOMPSON

Oak Tree Media Group
Books for Life

For Bulk Sales Contact:
MOVING BEYOND MINISTRIES
816-292-2846
Email us at: Info@MovingBeyondMinistries.Com

Jesus Girl - Doing Real Life!

Edited by Michael David McGuire
Interior Design by Steve Plummer
Cover Design by Media Consulting Services, New York
Cover Photos by Carolyn Doerflinger
Printed in the USA

ISBN 978-0-9864095-0-9

*"I have come that they may have life...
and that they may have it more abundantly."*

-Jesus of Nazareth
(John 10:10)

TABLE OF CONTENTS

ACKNOWLEDGMENTS
AMAZING PEOPLE IN MY LIFE

IT HAS GIVEN me great joy to actually hold a loose leaf, typed draft copy of this book in my hands. I now know just how long and difficult the process is for actually writing a book. I now know the amount of effort and human spirit that goes into the process...and I have a far greater appreciation for all who have had the courage to put their innermost personal feelings and failures in writing as a way to share a faith-based inspirational message with others.

I could not have undertaken this project without God's Good Guidance and the love and support of my husband Joe. I also want to offer very special thanks to my media advisor Michael David McGuire and his team in New York. He, too, is a firm believer in the power of prayer and I know in my heart this project might never has been completed without his advice, encouragement and tough guiding hand.

To my dear friend Shani Dorsey, who literally and figuratively held my hand through some of the very darkest days of my life, I offer my lifelong appreciation. She, more than anyone, knows the depth of my pain at that time...and knows that without her help at that very darkest moment I might not be here at all.

To Mike and Linda Brown, I hold you up to people worldwide as an example of God's Love for a Stranger. Your simple act of offering a helping hand, a Christian home and loving, parent-like advice when it was most needed, gave me the guidance and stability that allowed me to take charge of getting my own life back on track. If each of us, as Christians, can find a way within our means and ability to help our fellow humans as Mike and Linda Brown helped me and as I know they have helped others...we could eliminate hunger, drug addiction and homelessness in our nation almost overnight.

To everyone else who has been part of this story...and you know who you are because we have broken bread together...I express my deep appreciation for your guidance, help, friendship and life lessons. You all also know that the names in this book have been changed, primarily to avoid embarrassment to those who are shown in a light that is not very attractive.

And finally...with sincerity and great humility...I also say thanks to those in this story who represent the not so positive influences in my life, since the human flaws and fragilities represented by your part of this story helped give me the strength to overcome my own failings and the insights to share those failings with others. I pray for your salvation and know that you, too, will one day be forgiven... at the exact moment you ask God for that forgiveness.

PROLOGUE TO MY STORY

PASTOR BARRY YOUNG

I N WRITING A personal story like this... about the failings in one's life... one could start the story almost anywhere. In reading the completed manuscript for this book, I realized that I owe so much to Pastor Barry Young, my personal Mentor in Christ. As I faced the darkest and most desperate days of the part of my life that I share in this book... and as I made the conscious decision to turn my life to Christ... Pastor Barry gave me a written list of Five Simple Steps one can take to have a better life. Once I began to implement those steps in my life, I began to see my life change virtually over night. I have carried those five steps with me... everywhere I go and have gone... for the past eight years... on the same piece of paper Pastor Barry gave me that day. I share that list with you here so that it can help enrich your life and so that you can then share this list with others so that it may also enrich their lives.

I. WALK Closely w/ God
- Daily Prayer
- Daily Reading the Bible
- Church Attendance

II. DON'T SETTLE
- in relationships
- in money
- in education

III. GET STABLE

IV. When you can Leave do it

V. Get the trash out

FIVE SIMPLE STEPS
FROM PASTOR BARRY YOUNG

STEP ONE - WALK CLOSELY WITH GOD

DAILY PRAYER - It's important to find a time to be quiet and seek God. This is a time to communicate with Him. Just you and Him. God allows us to go directly to Him...we have open access any day, any time. Just like a close personal friend, how can we possibly get to know someone if we don't spend time with them?

Daily reading of the Bible- The Bible is God's Spoken Word, His promises, His provision for your life. How do you know His Word if you don't read it?

Attend Church - It is extremely important to be surrounded with like-minded people. People who will build you up, not tear you down. God did not call us to go through life's struggles alone. There are so many wonderful churches and wonderful people ready to embrace you and help you. Church is a refuge, a place of healing.

STEP TWO - DON'T SETTLE

In relationships
In Money
In Education
The bottom line is God wants the very best for you … and has your very best interests in mind. Don't settle for second best or mediocre. Maybe it's a job, a dead beat boyfriend or friends who are leading you down an un-Godly path. If you hate your job, take classes to learn something you'll like better. If its money problems, learn better money management. If it is a troubled marriage, seek counseling. Don't settle for what's not working.

STEP THREE - GET STABLE

Get stable in your mind, stable in your relationships and stable in your emotions. Get stable in your work and stable with your finances. Get stable with your home life and stable with your living environment. Get stable with your health. Get stable with your schedule, your exercise and your sleeping patterns.

STEP FOUR - LEAVE WHEN YOU CAN

If you are in an abusive relationship, leave when you can. If you work at a job you don't like or in a business run by an abusive boss...leave when you can. God does not want you to be stuck anywhere...and He wants you to know that you have the power to leave.

For some, it may not necessarily be about physically leaving a place. It may be more about leaving behind a bad situation, a bad emotion or a bad state of mind by making a change. If something is not working in your life...leave it behind.

STEP FIVE - GET THE TRASH OUT

We all have had trash, garbage or extra baggage in our lives that weighs us down and holds us back from meeting God's Best Plan for our lives. Get rid of it…take it out…kick it to the curb! The ugly spoken words, the voices of negativity, the gossiping tongue, the verbal abuse, the lies about others. Throw it all away…get it gone!

And now my story begins…

JESUS GIRL
Doing Real Life!

CANCER DIAGNOSIS
CHAPTER ONE

THERE ARE MOMENTS in one's life where everything becomes laser focused and sharp…moments that will stick in one's memory forever. That hot August day in Phoenix was one such moment…and is the moment that God showed me I should begin this story.

Phoenix is not a bad place, but, quite frankly, it is not on the list of the world's most beautiful cities. The day was dusty, dry and smoggy. PHX, the Phoenix Airport, is called Sky Harbor International and is actually pretty nice as airports go. There are nice shops, healthy food and clean restrooms. I had almost finished my bible college studies and was on my way to Los Angeles for a Jesus Culture Conference.

Two rows over, a mom and daughter read a book together. On the other side of the hall, an old black man stooped over a drinking fountain…and a group of college students ran quickly to their next flight. I was looking for a quiet corner to return the phone call from Julie, Dr. Adams' personal nurse, before boarding our 9:25 flight to LAX.

Julie was not her usual cheery self when she took my call. I can't explain the exact difference, but you must know what I mean when I write that my internal guidance told me that this would not be a routine call. When Dr. Adams came on the line, his words surpassed even my worst imaginable fears.

"Andrea, your tests are back. There's no easy way to say this. I'm very sorry. It's cervical cancer." I felt as if I'd been hit over the head with a two-by-four. This horrific news was coming from a guy who was not only my doctor, but from a man who had become like a friend over the past 20 years. His style was very professional and blunt, which I always appreciated. He tried his best to be reassuring and kind…but, in my mind and to my ears, everything translated to "you are going to die."

How could I tell Morgan? How could I tell Dalton? How could I let my kids know that their mom was going to die? How could I fly to LA? How do I interact with other people? Do I fake it? Do I attempt to smile? Do I cry? Do I fight? Do I just give up? Dear God…I prayed…what do I do?

What about the conference? What about my mom? What about my dad? Would he even really care? Who gets my stuff? How do I pay for all of this? Will it hurt? Where do I start? The thoughts and images that swirled through my mind were fast, furious and confusing in a way that only those who have stared death in its very real face could ever possibly even begin to understand. Do I start planning a funeral? Who's going to do the dishes? Will Morgan's dad get custody? And what about Joe...the new guy in my life? It seemed to me that this kind of news would be the ultimate deal breaker...and Dear God...Joe seemed so right.

I bit my lip and walked towards the boarding gate. Out of the blue, I thought about Jason. What was I going to tell Jason?

A VERY BAD BOY
CHAPTER TWO

THE TRUTH WAS I came to despise Jason. Sure, I loved him at first and there was even a time when he was a good father to our kids, but his ongoing deceit and irresponsibility changed all that. Yes, I understood the concept of forgiveness. And, intellectually, I know that God wants us to forgive, which is His ultimate gift to us, but I wasn't quite there yet.

Knowing all of this in my mind is one thing, but knowing this…really knowing it…in one's heart is quite another matter. But, at that moment…in the swirling confusion of the boarding area at PHX…all I could see was Jason's beady little eyes in his callous round face and my mind's replay of his lies, negativity and humiliation that I let him place on me.

As I walked those four feet to the gateway, it was as if I had entered a time warp where thirty years of my life had been compressed into no more than 90 seconds. Yes, I was strong. Yes, I was a survivor. Yes, I was a fighter…and, yes, I had Jesus on my side. I would not let this cancer beat me, and that's what I would say to Morgan, Dalton, my Mom, Joe…and even to my special new friend in Topeka, KS who so openly shared her life's story with me that fall day.

DEALING WITH BAD BOYS

CHAPTER THREE

THERE ARE THINGS we know in our heads...our intellectual self...that we may not yet know in our hearts. Jason did really bad things to me. He lied to me, he cheated on me, he used me. He manipulated my feelings and raped me emotionally...which sticks in my mind as the worst humiliation of all.

I knew...intellectually...that Jason did not do those things to me, but that I let him do those things and that I, personally, had to take responsibility. Knowing that concept of personal responsibility in one's head is one thing, however, knowing that concept...and I mean really knowing it...in one's heart is something totally different. I now know I had not yet fully grasped that concept...in my heart...until that autumn day when I met Pearl at the Women's Connection Summit.

Pearl was, I would guess, in her eighties. She was well-mannered, well-groomed, upright, prim and proper in that "perfect life" kind of mid-west way. She was towards the back of the line of about twenty or so similarly dressed blue-haired ladies who came up to shake my hand after my presentation. Pearl stood out and I sensed that she had something really important to share.

Pearl told me that she had never told her story to any other person before. Somehow she felt that she could...and needed...to confide her story in me. Pearl had grown up on a farm, the youngest of six kids...an outwardly normal life. But, after her mom died, the scene changed behind closed doors. For two years, from the time she was ten to twelve, she was raped repeatedly by her father and there was no one to tell.

For seventy years, Pearl had carried this dark and heavy secret...fully expecting to take it with her to the grave. However, that day, for the first time in seventy years, she knew that God had given her permission to open up...to finally tell her story...and forgive. At that moment she cried and told me that for the first time in years she felt free.

I hugged her...and at that moment I forgave Jason, too. Not just in my head...intellectually...but also in my heart. Just as Jesus has forgiven each and every one one of us. Jason was a jerk, Jason will most likely always be a jerk...but I had taken that burden from my heart and, at that very moment, I forgave. And that gift of forgiveness was sparked by Pearl in Topeka on that crisp, cloudy day. I felt alive, I felt free...and there were so many things I wanted to go back in time to tell me; my younger self.

LESSONS FOR YOUNGER ME
CHAPTER FOUR

As I FILLED my head with things to tell the younger me...one word popped to the top of the list. That word was "run". Notice that the word was not discuss, contemplate, explore...or think about it. The word is "run".

As I sat down for the conversation with my younger self, I realized that the advice I was giving would be good advice for anyone...daughter, granddaughter, next-door neighbor or niece. I wondered, at that time, why we so often lack the courage to speak to those who most need the advice. What I learned...and what I shared with the young me that day...was really very simple and obvious.

If anyone in your life...especially a new boyfriend or lover or husband...tries to manipulate you to be something other than your true self, run. If anyone tries to make you something that you are not, run. If anyone...anywhere, anytime...tries to trick you into going against your own best judgement, run. No man, no relationship, no job...no nothing…is worth the price of compromising your soul or changing your own true self.

In my mind, my younger self relished this guidance and advice…but I knew that hard conversation with real world, today young people might honestly take a good bit more courage. Would I really have the courage to say what needed to be said? Now I do, but a few years ago…I doubt if I did.

You see, Jason really was quite something. He was strong, he was handsome…he was a charmer. He was the first man to really pay attention to me and to pay attention to my feelings. He was a man who could be a father and a husband…we could build a family. Sure, there were lies…but, at least at first, they were just "little lies". And I was dumb and naive enough to let them slip without challenge, which is the point I should have ran!

As I sat there that afternoon with my younger self, the wisdom of more age and maturity allowed me to see and share the obvious, which is…so-called "little lies" are always a cover for or introduction to the Big Lies. And with Jason, the Big Lies turned out to be drug use, drug addiction and open infidelity. He used my dependance on him…and the fact that I did not run…to manipulate my mind, my body and my spirit to please his own selfish needs and wants. And I was stupid and blind enough to let him do it. I did not walk away. I did not run!

"But people can change, can't they?" I heard the younger me ask. "Yes, they can," I answered, "but never if they have no intention of changing, and never if they've turned their back on God's Truth, Integrity and Trust."

In looking back, I see so much more clearly now. Yes...it's really terrible when people lie to you, but it is doubly terrible when you start lying to yourself. With Jason, I was letting myself buy into really big lies. Lies that went against my very grain, lies that went against my soul...lies that let me turn my back on Jesus.

FALSE CHANGES
CHAPTER FIVE

I N GOD'S EYES…each and every one of us is born perfect, in His own image. Yet societal pressure and media images make us think that we need to do something to make ourselves "better". We need to be skinnier, more muscular…have a smaller nose, a bigger butt, redder lips, curlier hair…or straighter hair, lighter lips and a smaller butt. Our eyes are either too big or too small and our skin is either too white or too dark.

In my relationship with Jason, I received the attention I so craved from a man, but it came at a terrible price. I turned my back on God and God's true plan for me. God had made me perfect, however, to get the attention from Jason…ultimately a false attention…I thought I needed to change everything about me. I dieted to the point of near starvation. I became an unnatural blonde and I had surgical breast implants to "please" my man, while neither

JESUS GIRL - Doing Real Life!

pleasing me nor God. I became a skinny blonde...with the breasts that Jason wanted...and I was miserable.

At the time, it seemed like I was making only "little compromises" to give my husband the woman he wanted. But, in reality, I was doing exactly the opposite. Big Lies and Big Deceit start with little lies and little "compromises" that turn our own true selves away from God's True Purpose for us and our lives. As obvious as that seems to me now, it was not obvious to me then...nor is it obvious to many of the women I meet as I travel across the country. We as women are often taught that we have to be the ones making the changes to make life, relationships, homes and marriages work. If the change follows God's Great Plan, then change is good. If those changes are forced upon us to please another...and go against what is good in God's eyes...then that change is both false and bad. The heartfelt stories I have heard can still make me cry.

14

REJECTING FALSE CHANGE
CHAPTER SIX

I HAVE ALWAYS THOUGHT of myself as a strong person. Like so many others, I have faced terrible adversity in relationships, child rearing, health and finances. But, as I look back over my life, every one of those adversities have made me stronger…and every one of those challenges were solved by listening quietly to God's Good Guidance.

In my work as a minister and speaker, I hear many stories. I do not want to minimize any single story, but this drama we call life almost always plays out with only minor script variations. Troubled children, a straying husband, lost job, disease or death of a loved one. But on some occasions, when speaking to groups, I hear a story that will make me cry later that night, alone in my hotel room.

In Simi Valley, CA, I met a new bride named Monica. She was very much in love with her groom and had tied the knot only three months earlier. Monica was feeling uncomfortable because the foundation of their newlywed sex lives had begun to change significantly since getting married. Her husband, who I will call Jeff, had unpacked two boxes of pornographic videos in their new bedroom. Jeff had favorites, which he wanted Monica to watch. He would then want her to play act with him and replicate the on screen action. This made Monica extremely uncomfortable, but she had been taught to be a good and obedient wife, a role she felt duty bound to fulfill. How could she find the strength to adjust to this new reality? My answer, of course, was that God would NEVER require anyone to make this type of False Change. If Monica's new husband truly loved her, then he would love her as God loved her. Since God had already made her perfect, there was no need or requirement for her to become some on-screen porno queen.

Then there was Tammy in Austin, TX who received the fastest answer of anyone that day. Tammy's latest boyfriend kept insisting that she try a little ecstasy every time they went dancing at late night raves. Tammy insisted she was not into drugs and really resented the pressure. I asked Tammy if she felt that doing drugs was part of how God made her. Her answer was "no." "Easy, then," I said, "no False Changes for anyone."

Story after story...state after state...meeting after meeting...the tragedies played out. But the bottom-line real problem...in almost every instance...is that people had turned their life from God.

A SLAP UPSIDE THE HEAD
CHAPTER SEVEN

As I METAPHORICALLY sat down for my weekly chat with my younger self...as part of the process in writing this book...I decided to include a cup of green tea. As we relaxed...girl-to-girl...my younger self slipped into an argumentative and challenging mood.

"But, doesn't God want us to grow...to try new things... to make changes that make our lives better?" the younger me asked, knowing, of course, that she had me in a corner.

"Yes, of course," I answered. "But the key phrase in your question is 'make our lives better'. False Changes go against our core spirit, our core value and our core selves. If it is not good in God's eyes, then that specific change is not good for you."

"But how do I tell the difference?" the younger me asked. "A little kid might not like eating broccoli, but changing their diet to include broccoli would actually be a good change."

Good point, I thought. I sipped my tea to contemplate the single best answer. "If your own internal guidance makes you uncomfortable, the change requested is most likely not a good idea. If the requested change seems to offer only selfish benefit or pleasure to another...it will most likely prove to not be good for you. If a change involves a reshaping of your personality or physical self...think very long and hard before proceeding."

"That boils down to discernment," a clear statement from the younger me...and a good point. I could tell she was catching on, which made me feel really proud. I could also tell that the younger me appreciated the thoughtfulness of my advice, which I knew was very much spot on and exactly the kind of advice I wish that I would have received in reality when I was younger...advice to help counter the really ugly, negative and hurtful things I heard from my own father.

DADDY DEAREST
CHAPTER EIGHT

As I sat down to write this book, I struggled most with this chapter. My dad was not a bad man, per se. But he was a man…like many other men…who either knowingly or unknowingly did bad things. To call what he did to me a crime is maybe too harsh a word, but it is a word I will use within the context of this book to convey what I see as the serious nature of neglect and verbal abuse perpetrated by men on their wives and young daughters…a "crime" that passes from generation to generation…and over the years, hurts so many.

We as women learn how to be treated by men from our fathers. How our fathers treat our mothers…and us as young girls…has a profound impact on the choices we make in choosing a mate…in choosing our men… later in life.

With my dad, I remember being a little girl and enjoying the attention he would show me. I remember "fun family times" and softball games. I remember rare, affectionate and important embraces as a little girl. This was all positive affirmation, which is very important to a young child. However, what I remember even more was his verbal put-downs related to my physical appearance, my weight and my development as a young woman. These ongoing messages were subtle, pervasive and very effective...teaching me, as so many other women have been taught, that to get the positive attention and affection of a man...one had to reshape her body, reshape her mind and reshape her approach to life to fit a certain mold.

To make one's own decisions...to focus on one's own God-given inner strength...and not focus on outward physical appearance...was to lose daddy's approval and daddy's love. Which then sets a pattern of changing and adjusting our focus on outward appearance that then leads us, as women, to be manipulated based on awards (financial incentives) and rewards (a man's affection) to change who we are on both the inside and the outside. And this goes completely against God's True Nature.

OUR BAD CHOICES
CHAPTER NINE

I HAVE MET...and I continue to meet...hundreds of people as I travel this nation with our ministry. I am convinced that the vast majority of people, and at this moment I speak specifically to women...do not set out intentionally to make bad choices, but that pervasive and subtle training by our untrained and unthinking fathers trains us subliminally to make ongoing and pervasive bad choices about men and relationships with men.

If, as a little girl, we get more of daddy's attention (love) when we are skinny by constantly being told how much better we look with less weight...then we may, as women, go to extremes to meet a pre-determined, self-imposed body image to attract a man, to get his attention and to get his love. In extremes, this can lead to starvation diets, laxatives, bulimia and other unhealthy and stressful eating disorders.

The same applies to issues of hair color, personal

attitudes, personality, opinions and breast size. As offensive and controversial as this point may be to some, I invite my dear readers to stop and think about the impact…and truth…of what I write.

We are taught…in a pervasive, effective and subliminal way…to adjust our thoughts and conversation to align with the men in our lives. If we have a thought or an idea that is "counter" to the family's best direction…for example, the man's thought and/or definition of best interest…we are trained to keep our mouths shut and not share our inner thoughts, emotions or suggestions.

The same goes with physical appearance. If one can just be a blonde…or a redhead or a brunette…or anything else other than what God gave us…our man will, we falsely think, like us better and we will get more awards and rewards…even if it goes against God's Great Plan. We are taught at a very early age to be quiet, to be agreeable…to be skinnier…to get bigger boobs…and your life with your man will be great! Except, of course, when one honestly realizes that outward physical appearance, when done to please and/or impress another, will never please one's own self and will never please God.

TALKING TO DADDY'S GIRL
CHAPTER TEN

W HEN I SAT down to talk with the younger me for this chapter...I noticed that she was about five years younger than she had been in the earlier chapter. I asked the younger me how old she was on this specific day...and she told me almost twelve. She knew ahead of time what we were going to discuss...and I could tell that she was uncomfortable, as was I. I picked a place with happy memories of our dad, on a little dock over the waters of Lake Cachuma where we went fishing when I was little. The younger me knew I had picked this spot for a very specific reason.

Talking with our sons and daughters about really tough issues is always uncomfortable...sometimes more so for the parent than for the child. The level of discomfort is so great that many parents avoid these discussions altogether...leaving the most critical childhood development issues to strangers or inexperienced and misguided childhood friends and schoolmates. This was the case with my parents and, at that moment, I must confess that I was a bit nervous having this conversation now with my younger self.

"It's a bit warmer here than I remember," the younger me said with a bit of hesitation in her voice.

"Yeah," I agreed, knowing that we had more important things to discuss. There was a bit more awkward silence, then I jumped in.

"You know, many parents are never available to their kids, which was certainly the case with our dad." The almost twelve-year-old me nodded. "And then, when parents make themselves available, they sometimes are way too critical...way too judgmental...and don't take the time to listen." Again the younger me nodded.

"I know dad used to love me," the young me said, "but I feel now as if I've been left all alone because I am not pretty enough to be his daughter." Her pain was obvious...as her eyes began to fill with tears. I knew her pain...I could relate very directly to that pain...because that was my pain as a young girl so many years ago.

The flood of emotions, for both of us, was overwhelming. I heard me...the older me...saying out loud the ugly mantra that I knew the younger me had played in my own head before. "I'm not good enough...I'm not smart enough...I'm not pretty enough...I'm not worthy enough...to be my dad's daughter." Tears rolled down the cheeks of the younger me. Memory tears welled in my eyes, too.

"But you now know that none of that is true...don't you?" I asked the younger me, wiping my own tears as she wiped hers. "Those are feelings that we let our dad put on us...and he could put those feelings on us because he never had guidance on how to honestly care for and love another human being." This was almost too weighty a concept for the twelve-year-old me to fully grasp, but it helped me feel better to at least verbalize what the older me could now grasp and understand.

As I wiped my tears with a tissue from my purse, the younger me had vanished, leaving me with the first sense of real peace I had felt about my dad...and my relationship with him. The lesson came to me as an epiphany...it seemed so obvious and so right...yet it had been so many painful years in coming.

Just because a young girl...or a young boy...is physically and/or emotionally abandoned by their worldly father...our Heavenly Father has been there, is there and will be there forever. At that moment I was filled with the most spectacular sense of joy and amazement I had experienced in a very long time. This realization...this amazing shining light of an idea...helped me see so very clearly why and how I had made the mistakes that I had stumbled into for so many years. It showed me why I had made so many bad choices. It showed me why I had stumbled in so many bad relationships. It allowed me to begin the process of healing and...maybe most importantly of all...it allowed me finally to forgive my earthly, biological dad for all he had done to me, my mother and my sister.

As I packed up to leave the shores of Lake Cachuma, I knew that I would be seeing the younger me again in the next few days, although the younger me was not present when I received this final, shining lesson, I knew that she would get that same gift later because, after all, she was me and I am now her. Both of us are now blessed with the gift of forgiveness, including forgiving our earthly father for his shortcomings and knowing without a doubt that our Heavenly Father had never...and would never...abandon us. What a powerful and joyful lesson to share with others!

JEWISH GIRL MEETS JESUS
CHAPTER ELEVEN

JESUS ALWAYS SOUNDED to me like a pretty good guy. He was cool, handsome...had great long hair...and great advice for everyone. I could dig on the message of peace and love. But I realize now that I didn't really know anything...not really. My knowledge of Jesus was based on stories I heard in school...and the blue-eyed Protestant painting I had seen as a young girl hanging on the wall of a friend's home.

As a minister, as I travel around the world, people often ask how I met Jesus. They ask me to tell my personal story of forgiveness and salvation, which, of course, I love to share. The truth is that my personal story is not unlike stories one might hear from others, but my story has always had a rather unique twist.

Although I was born into a Jewish household, neither of my parents were very religious, although they did give show to some of the Jewish holidays, like Rosh

Hashanah, Yom Kippur and Hanukkah, which we nominally celebrated each year. On the other hand, I couldn't even begin to tell you the traditions associated with Shavuot, Sukkot and Puram.

My mother, who really liked celebrations, was always really big on holidays, any holiday. She always made a point to make them special. She put a lot of effort into the food, the decorations and the warm feelings of the occasion. We even celebrated Christmas and had Easter baskets in the spring. My father mostly went along for the ride, although he really wasn't a big fan.

I honestly can't say if my parents' exploration of "religion" was from an honest curiosity…a desire to expose me to a wider world…or just a way to fill in family time on Saturdays and Sundays. We tried going to a conservative synagogue one Saturday…but the door was locked. Next, we tried Hillcrest Christian Church, where there was a pastor my parents really admired. I was registered at Hillcrest Christian elementary school for fourth grade, where I continued to learn about this good-guy named Jesus. His picture was on the wall of every room…and everyone talked about trying to live their life as He would. For me, at age eight, these were interesting concepts that filled me with great curiosity.

In my young eyes, here was a guy who could turn water into wine, multiply bread and fish to feed thousands…and, best of all, he could even walk on water. This was the point, the personal characteristic of Jesus, that stuck in my mind at the top of the list...at least for me at that time in life.

The more I learned, the closer I felt to the ideas and ideals of Jesus. Even as an eight year old girl, I could see that Jesus, as a man, stood by what he said. I could see that He helped sick people. I could see that He helped hungry people...and I could see that He even helped kids who were being bullied, which was really good news for a young girl like me.

As this new relationship came over me, I felt such joy...and, I now must admit, I felt somewhat smug, because I was learning things that I assumed many of the people in my life...including my parents...did not know. This made me feel somewhat smarter and better than most of those around me...or so I thought. It wasn't until years and years of heartache and struggle later that I saw just how wrong I was. Sure, I knew Jesus. However at this point, I realize now, I knew Jesus in my head...but not in my heart.

THE BIGGEST HYPOCRITE
CHAPTER TWELVE

SMUG PEOPLE ARE not attractive...and if that is a true statement, then I must have been a somewhat ugly little girl at that point in my life. I saw hypocrisy and hypocrites everywhere...and I was often the first to judge.

Mrs. Brown was the school librarian, but I knew that she smoked cigarettes. She snuck outside during lunch and, worst of all, she even smoked while driving. In my young judging eyes...that hardly made her a Christian.

Old Mr. Mackey had a store downtown. His son was on the high school football team and he won a scholarship to college, but I knew that Mr. Mackey sometimes didn't pay for newspapers. How Christian was that? He could brag on his son for football...when behind the scenes, he might be a thief. What would Jesus think?

Then there was Missy Taylor at the grocery store...who everyone said drank beer on the weekends. She would be at Church almost every Sunday, but secretly I knew that everyone said she might be an alcoholic. So...how could she ever say that she really knew Jesus?

Yes...in those days, I certainly knew Jesus in my head...but not in my heart. In looking back, as if getting slapped in the face with a cold, slimy fish...I realize now that I was the biggest hypocrite of all. How was I going to tell this lesson to the younger me?

GUIDE FOR THE YOUNGER ME
CHAPTER THIRTEEN

WHEN I SHOWED up at the tea house for that afternoon's outing with the younger me, I saw that the "younger me" was a bit more grown up than I was expecting. She had more of an air of young sophistication than I had seen before...but it was that false sophistication that one sees in those who are only fifteen.

"Hey, good seeing you again," the now older "younger me" said.

"Yes," I said, "I am glad you could come."

"So...what's the lesson for today?" she asked. I felt myself getting terribly uncomfortable, because I had been expecting a much younger "younger me" and had mentally prepared for an age appropriate discussion, which I felt confident I could handle quite well. Now...faced with the older "younger me"...I was thrown off base because I was now forced to talk about my own hypocrisy in a more grownup, adult way.

"Hey, look at that loser," the younger me said, pointing towards another girl about her age who had just come in. I looked over and recognized the girl as a girl who I had know from school when I, too, was fifteen. "You should see her at school," the younger me said, as my own memories came flooding back. "She's pregnant, you know." I realized then just how smug and obnoxiously hypocritical I had been. It seemed hopeless. And at that point...as much as I hate to admit it...I did exactly what so many parents do when dealing with teenagers and sensitive issues. I ducked...and I told the younger me that I wanted her to read Chapter Fourteen of my new book.

ON TO STRIPPING
CHAPTER FOURTEEN

I T WAS JASON, my boyfriend, who got me into stripping. Imagine the worst and that was it...half-naked
on stage, a pole...and obnoxious, drunk older men, slob-
bering on themselves and giving me lots of money.

In the beginning, I was actually too young to be
working in the club, but getting the fake ID was easy.
So was the mind transformation I put myself through to
justify my actions. I was stripping to please Jason, I was
stripping to prove that I could make it financially on my
own and that I could have power over men and make
good money in the process. Jason was turned on by the
idea that I was stripping...and I was turned on by Jason.

Frank, the club manager, was my guide and my pro-
tector through this underground culture. He watched
out for me and made certain that no one got out of
hand. After all, I was his new star...and it was the new
stars who got the drunks to roll in and spend money. In

some small ways, Frank was a saint. And with that one statement...you can see just how twisted I allowed my head to get.

In writing this book, I have poured out my soul. I've had to face the facts and the reality of my past life. Some of my life is not pretty and some readers may be offended. Some may think that the lessons are over simplified. But I know in my heart that, for whatever reason, these are the stories and lessons that God wants me to share with the world. This is not an easy process...I sometimes worry about the judgement of others...but this is what I was shown to do.

It is so easy in life to make one small compromise... that then leads to the next small compromise...which leads to even bigger compromises...and, before long, we find ourselves a totally different person and totally lost. Sometimes that fog is so thick we ourselves do not know that we've lost our way. Much like me at that time dancing half naked in front of sloppy, ogling drunks. I was addicted to the money...and Jason was hot for the game.

TOUGH STORIES
CHAPTER FIFTEEN

A T THE STRIP club, Frank would keep an eye on the customers, the customers kept their eyes on me...and I kept my eye on Jason, who didn't really have a job. Jason was really turned on by me, his girlfriend, working as a dancer...but it began to seem to me that he was even more interested in the money I was making showing off my body.

Jason would come by the club, usually about 10:00pm, and wait outside with the bouncer until I could take my next break. He was always broke...he always needed a little extra cash for whatever...which I was happy to provide because in my screwed up head, I thought I loved him. However, after awhile, this one way money street was getting old and Frank was sharp enough to smell things before me.

Frank was heavyset...Italian...with a no-bull, military kind of personality. He showed me the ropes and acted as my professor. At first, I didn't understand why he didn't like Jason...until the night he suggested I run over to the Pussy Kat, another strip club, about a mile away. This was just after Jason had stopped by to pick up three hundred bucks he said he needed for a special model train his friend wanted to sell. I asked Frank what was up...and all he said was "Honey, I really think you ought to go." He seemed really serious...so I got in the car and drove over to the Pussy Kat on my break.

As I walked into the club, Steve at the front door wasn't as friendly as he had been before. I spotted Maury, the manager, who looked nervous when he saw me come in. As my eyes adjusted to the dim strip club lights, the same bump-de-bump music blared and the place was half filled with some of the same faces from our club...including Jason who was sitting down front giving twenty dollar bills to the topless Michelle, who I knew from when she worked at our place. Michelle saw me right away, but drunk Jason was oblivious to anything except his own immediate titillation.

As I walked towards the front of the club, several of the clients recognized me...even fully dressed with my coat on. Michelle pulled herself away from Jason and walked towards the dressing room. At that point, Jason saw me and looked startled, like a baby deer in the headlights. "Hey, Honey," he managed to say, then jumped up and ran straight into the men's bathroom. I followed, banging on the locked door until he opened it. I was shocked, sad and furious. I looked at Jason...and he just stood there like some scared kid. "Honey, really! It has nothing to do with you." I could have slugged him, but held back.

I grabbed what was left of my money that he still clasped in his fist, then turned and walked towards the front door with as much dignity as I could muster. Of course, in retrospect, there wasn't much dignity in any of this scene. The reality of my life was not good. I was an underage stripper...getting half-naked for strange men...so that the "love of my life" could take my money...and give it to other naked women. How sad and sick was that?

TOUGH LOVE
CHAPTER SIXTEEN

A PARENT NEEDS TO know the difference between tough love and just being tough. Sometimes, I think some parents offer what they think is "tough love" just to show mindless dominance or to cover up their own deep-seated insecurities. At this point in my life, I pray that I know the difference.

I had scheduled my meeting with the younger me for an early Thursday afternoon. I had received a note from her saying that she had read Chapter Fourteen. My heart sank a bit because that was all she wrote. No sense of curiosity…no sense of shock…no acknowledgement that she (the younger me) turned out to be a stripper in some dank, dark club.

As I waited for the younger me to show up that Thursday afternoon, the waiter brought rolls and butter. I asked for more iced tea…and I mentally rehearsed the wise lessons I would offer that day. The more I thought, however, the more unsure I became about my well-laid plan. The clock ticked by an hour…then ninety minutes…and I was still waiting.

Perform a good show, be quiet, smile…and get paid. Frank taught me that on my first day at the club. As offensive as this next statement may be to some…is that not how many women let themselves be subjugated? Create the show of a lovely home, don't complain if your husband ignores your needs…and just smile on the outside; when all you really want to do is cry.

How sad, I thought. Then I realized…this is the core message I would share with the younger me. But, more than two hours on…and three glasses of iced tea later…I knew that I'd been stood up. The younger me just didn't want to deal with the "now me" that day.

THE REALITY OF RAPE
CHAPTER SEVENTEEN

THERE WERE DAYS in my life where I really didn't want to get out of bed or even deal with me, at least the way my head was then. For the first time, the younger me had stood the older me up for one of our pre-arranged meetings. I was feeling insecure about this process and my advice, much the same as any parent feels sometimes when dealing with their child. How can we...as parents...give advice when we know in our own hearts that we ourselves were not ...and are not...perfect?

As I did laundry that day, I ran everything through my mind...trying to understand what I gained by sharing the story about having been a stripper. By sharing that story...do I gain friends? Do I lose friends? Will people walk away? Will I lose credibility with my own grown kids? Will I lose credibility with my ministry? I prayed, and in my heart, God told me, "Get over it."

Reality is reality…and truth is truth. The more we acknowledge our realities…both the realities of our past and of our current day…the faster we get to our own personal truth. And the faster we get to a real, deep and honest truth, the closer we are personally to God and the faster we can help others get closer to God, too.

When I became an underage stripper, I did so thinking that I was making my own grownup decision, but in reality, I was allowing myself to be manipulated by others. I was being manipulated by my own unhealthy relationship with my father…which, in turn, generated the manipulative relationship with Jason, who in some twisted way, I thought I loved. If the younger me didn't want to face me that day…for whatever reason…that was her decision and quite frankly, her loss. It was also a chance, I realized as I put the washed clothes into the dryer, to better focus my message. For me, that laundry day, the message was…"Honey, speak up!"

EMOTIONAL ABUSE IS RAPE
CHAPTER EIGHTEEN

MY FAMILY MADE it a show to "be a family." It was not until many years later that I realized that my mom tried her best...and was actually quite sincere in the effort...but my father was mostly uninvolved and only physically present, much like a community theatre actor walking through some scripted lines.

One family barbecue is seared into my mind. I was twelve-years-old and Uncle George was about thirty-five. He took me into the house to get a can of soda and told me there was something really important we needed to discuss in the back bedroom. It seemed odd to me even at the time that there was anything he would want to discuss with me...but he was Uncle George...and hey, it must be really important.

When we got to the spare bedroom, I realized then that it had to be really serious since he shut the door and locked it. He sat me down on the bed and put one arm around my shoulders, dangling his finger tips just above my young breast. His other hand landed up my leg and began to move upwards. I freaked out. "You must know I love you," he said.

I didn't know how to respond. I was confused. His hand continued its journey up my leg. His fingers reached my breast. I wanted to run, but was frozen in time and place...until my younger cousin knocked on the door, jiggled the door knob and told us lunch was ready.

Uncle George was startled, he stood up quickly, pulled himself together...unlocked and opened the door, then walked out as if nothing had happened. I followed...scared, confused and totally silent. And until this very moment, I never told that story to anyone.

Later, when I was fourteen...I found myself in another situation. My girlfriend Patsy dropped by one late afternoon to take me on a neighborhood adventure that was to include dropping by Tim's house, a ninth grader who was my latest semi-crush and lived just a couple of blocks away.

Tim came from a good family and lived in a really nice house. At first it was just Tim, Patsy and me hanging out, but then three of Tim's friends dropped by...followed by Dave and Derrick, two boys I knew from school, but who ran with a whole different crowd that Patsy didn't really like. Patsy decided to leave...and I made the mistake of deciding to stay because I trusted Tim.

At first it was just us seven kids hanging out. I began to feel awkward, however, when the vibe changed to six boys and one girl hanging out. I started to make my excuses about getting home for dinner...when suddenly the whole dynamic flipped in the twinkling of an eye. I was pushed into a dark room and forced onto an old mattress. Dave and Derrick led the way...Tim stood in the door and just watched. The other three boys didn't want to look weak and took their turn, too. I screamed and I cried, which did no good in that dark room...on that dirty mattress...on that day with those six boys.

Had I followed my own heart...had I been given some guidance on these sensitive matters...from my parents or grandparents...I would never have found myself in that situation. I would have spoken up. I would have followed my own gut instinct to run. But, as was expected of all girls in that day...and is still expected of many women today...I put on a good show when I arrived back home that evening. I pretended as if nothing extraordinary had happened. I was a good girl. I kept my mouth shut...and I kept on smiling.

DON'T BE A VICTIM
CHAPTER NINETEEN

THE YOUNGER ME sent a note apologizing for missing our scheduled meeting the week before. She admitted that she was a bit freaked out by my stripper story, but had read the next four chapters of the book and was curious to see what came next. She also pointed out that the chapter titles didn't completely match up with what I was writing in each specific chapter. She was correct because I wanted to save the real essence for our personal time together.

"Hey, sorry about last week," the younger me said when she sat down next to me on the park bench. It was a beautiful warm day...with just a few clouds over to the west. "So, what do we cover today?" she asked.

"Many things," I said with confidence.

"You told everyone in your book about what happened with Uncle George," she said, somewhat agitated. "We were supposed to keep that secret."

"Yes, I told everyone by writing the book," I said. "But you and I both should have spoken up at the time." The younger me nodded.

"How do you stop rape?" she asked. I sighed. The blunt answers that every loved one needs to share with their daughters began to flow.

"Almost 80% of all sexual violence against girls and women is committed by someone closest to them."

"What do you mean by closest?" the younger me asked.

"I mean…brothers, fathers, neighbor boys, boyfriends. Those who you trust and who you are around the most."

"Really?" she quizzed, somewhat concerned.

"Yes," I said, "those are the facts…and they are sometimes hard facts for women to believe. Like the fact that more than one in five women will face rape at some point in their lives. And…that 54% of rape victims never tell anyone."

"Just like us," the younger me said, as the reality of the truth dawned on her.

"Yes," I said. "Staying silent is wrong."

I turned my body to better face the younger me. "Not all boys are bad…but then, not all boys are good. You might be thinking about friendship and love, but most boys are only thinking about quick sex." The younger me seemed somewhat uncomfortable, but was listening. "If a boy really loves you…he will love and respect you without sex." The younger me nodded. "If sex is ever used as a tool, or a weapon, or a bribe…it's not good." I verbally marched on.

"Don't get in cars with groups of boys…and don't go into houses, bedrooms or basements with groups of boys, even if a boy you know is taking you." The pain in saying that last sentence hit me like a dagger in the heart because that is exactly what happened to me with Tim at his house. I really believed that Tim was my friend, but he didn't do anything at all to help me".

The younger me nodded and I saw the corner of her eyes get moist. "If only someone in my own life at that point would have had the courage to give me that simple advice…all of that would have been avoided." I could tell that the younger me was listening intently. I continued on.

"God gives every one of us the power to defend ourselves. Part of that wonderful tool is what I call a "gut feeling." Maybe its discernment, maybe its from the heart…but it's that quick spark in your gut that tells you something isn't right. Leave, run, get away."

"Okay," the younger me shook her head in agreement.

"Another part of that power is to NOT remain silent…but to speak up." I gestured forcefully as I spoke.

"And don't get in cars with boys," the younger me gestured back, with a slight laugh, a smile and a twinkle in her eyes, knowing that her simple statement was really acknowledgment and acceptance of a much wider lesson.

"Yes," I said. "That is the lesson."

"What about the idea that emotional abuse is as bad as rape?" she asked. "You titled that in one of your chapters."

"Actually," I corrected, "the chapter title read 'Emotional Abuse IS Rape", which is a much stronger statement."

"How so?" the younger me asked, as I looked at my watch, knowing that we had already gone past our scheduled time.

"Just read the next two chapters," I said. "I think the lessons in that story…as painful as they were for me at the time… actually play out quite well. You take the time to read…then you and I can cover the deeper lessons next week."

THE GIFT OF GOODBYE
CHAPTER TWENTY

FOR MANY PEOPLE...especially women...it is hard to grasp the concept that mental abuse can be even more traumatic than physical abuse...but this is scientific fact. While physical rape involves both a physical and a psychological attack...our brains cannot actually re-create the sensation of physical pain associated with the physical act. However, the psychological impact...the memory of the abuse...is so profound that it is often buried deep within one's psyche as a coping mechanism. This memory then plays in the background of our lives...impacting everything from that point on.

How many women do you know who love their husbands, love their children and work hard to provide the "perfect" home, yet endure verbal abuse on an almost daily basis? This abuse can take the form of yelling, screaming and/or verbal badgering. More often than not, however...each incidence is relatively minor, like a paper cut, that is then magnified by shear volume. Since we as women have been trained from early childhood to bury our own feelings in deference to the father, the boyfriend, the husband, the children and the "perfect" home...very few of us talk about these issues, so they remain a deep, dark secret. It is that personal secrecy which magnifies the negative impact on our lives...and plays out over and over like a bad TV re-run.

In my work as a minister, women tell me private stories that I am sure that some of them have never told any other human. Dinner is late, the house isn't clean, you've gained some weight, you forgot my shirts, you lost my socks, Molly at work looks really hot...I just don't find you attractive anymore. The stories come and the tears flow...not so much for any one small dig, but for the years and years of mental abuse piled one on top of the other...a constant undermining stream of negativity that destroys our very being much the same as dripping water can over time cut a stone.

When I was a little girl, my father told me he was going to send me to the "bad girls home" for punishment. He also told me...in very subtle ways...that I was not meeting his standard for beauty, weight or intelligence. Although I am sure that his intention was not to inflict verbal abuse...the abuse nonetheless cut me like a knife to the heart. I buried it deep and that choice set a pattern that impacted my life in very negative ways for many years to come...a pattern that had me changing who I was to please my biological father on the ground, without any guidance or regard for what was pleasing to my Heavenly Father above.

When I eventually married Jason, I realize now I did so to prove to him that I was worthy of his love, and like so many women, I just "knew" he would change with marriage. I know now my thinking was pretty naive. I also know just how familiar my own thoughts from those past days now sound to so many others...but I didn't see the pattern at the time. That pattern was the mindset that was placed on me as a young girl...which I then allowed myself to carry on into later life...which hurt me quite terribly.

In thinking back, I always hated that musty sweet smell of marijuana...but Jason was a dope smoker and I rationalized that it helped him relax after a stressful day. In retrospect, I have to laugh...since Jason rarely had a real job and I was the one supporting our home by working long nights taking my clothes off in front of strange men in a dimly lit room filled with smoke. As you read this book...does that not strike you as bizarre? Yet, this is how many of us let life play out...and fool ourselves...bit by tiny bit. It doesn't all happen in just one day. It happens because we bury our abuse deep inside...we look for approval...we try to please others...without giving thought to what pleases God.

When our son, Dalton, was born, I was so proud to be a new mom. Jason was proud, too. However, in retrospect, it strikes me that his pride was more male ego-centric and shallow. I set out to be the best mom I knew how to be and, for the most part, Jason tried to do the same. He was not a good breadwinner and as much as I wanted to give up the life of dancing in the clubs, I convinced myself that we needed the money to support our home and the new baby. I also conveniently convinced myself that there was no other option.

Jason was a selfish man and a superbly lousy husband. Yet, I was so busy trying to please him that I adjusted who I was and became blind to what was going on around me. Jason wanted me to play a certain sexy partner in bed. I did, although the act was not me and gave me no joy. Jason wanted me to enlarge my breasts. I didn't really want to have the surgery, but I did because it meant so much to Jason. He really liked the "new" girl...but that "new" girl really wasn't me...and certainly was not the me that God had created.

I completely lost sight of my own internal compass. I had married Jason for better or for worse...and for me, that meant forever and ever...no matter what. Had I been closer to God, I would have seen the red flags...the negative patterns...and the even bigger addiction. I certainly would have known God's Gift of Goodbye.

KNOWING WHEN TO LEAVE
CHAPTER TWENTY-ONE

As I worked late nights, I worked hard to support our family and to please Jason. Although I married Jason with the promise of monogamy, as he had so faithfully promised me...his definition of monogamy was not one any rational person could find in any dictionary anywhere. I even justified his little "flings" in much the same way a former president justified his as he humiliated himself and his wife in front of the nation.

At that time in my life, I had convinced myself that Jason loved me...because I so desperately wanted him to love me. I wanted his attention, his affection...and I wanted to please him. He promised to stop seeing other women, but that was a lie. He prowled the seedy strip clubs...even while I was dancing in a high class joint not far from our home. He told me more than once he laid off marijuana...yet still he almost always came home smelling like pot. I was sometimes furious with his ongoing deceit. I even threatened to leave him and our marriage more than once...but he and I both knew that was my lie.

I let my own mind trap me in a life that was not good...a life that was actively moving against my own creation...a life that was, without my conscious thought, not beneficial to my young son and most certainly not moving with God. The hole in my life and in my soul just kept getting deeper and deeper, but I was good at putting on a false happy face for the outside world...as the red flags continued to wave.

The next five years of my life were mostly a fast blur. I floated along dancing on and off at the club...making good money and supporting our home, our new son and thinking that I was being a good wife and a good mom by turning a blind eye to keep the marriage going. Jason, on the other hand, was truly good at manipulation, but not much else.

About the time I knew I was pregnant with our daughter Morgan, I wanted so desperately for me and Jason to work as a married couple and for him to step up and be the man of the house. I knew that pregnancy would put an end to my dancing career, and I was, quite frankly, worried about paying the bills.

During this time, Jason always managed to say the "right" things...but it seemed to me that he was losing interest. He was losing interest in me and losing interest in our marriage. I honestly tried hard to make things work. I tried by pleasing him. I tried because I so desperately...at a deep and hidden psychological level...needed his approval, needed his attention and needed his affection. I rationalized so much. His one-time "flings" with other women weren't really sex...it was just a physical release. Smoking dope wasn't like shooting heroin...or running down the street naked. However, his emotional and mental abuse was constant and ongoing and I felt like a rock that was about to be cut in half. Had I known God as I now know God...I would have understood the real Power of Prayer...and I would have prayed for guidance.

As the weeks strung out to months, I felt like I was surviving. I was being a good, quiet and obedient wife. I complained, but it did no good. I activated my blind eye and I was powering through...knowing in my clouded, secular heart that I was doing the best that I could for me, for Jason, for our son and for our new baby daughter, who was born that summer night. Through sheer ego and will...but without the guidance of God...I thought I could change Jason into the man he needed to be for all of our sake. At that point I was very sure I could succeed. That was also the point when I stumbled on the secret stash of hidden trash.

Even then I was not completely naive...and I knew that a lot of guys would look at porn from time-to-time. Jason's hidden stash, however, was bag after bag of well-worn magazines...a massive collection, hundreds of titles...and none of them were the vanilla style, regular sex Playboy pinups. The images were perverse, disturbing, and for me, quite frightening based on the images portrayed. They painted an ugly picture of a man disturbed...a man who I suddenly felt I could not trust!

As I dug deeper into Jason's nasty stash...my horror only grew. There were dozens and dozens of VHS tapes... and oddly strange sex toys that made me physically sick to my stomach. All of this painted Jason as a man who had a real disdain for women and a disregard for human life. A man that I did not want around my kids. How could I be married to a man who looked at this stuff? What were these bizarre videos about...what did he do with these things? This was sick and twisted. How could I let him touch me? Or...be around our children? I set myself to force a confrontation.

When Jason got back home that evening, he was furious that I had been going through his private treasures. I had already discretely wrapped everything...ready for the trash...but Jason grabbed my shoulders and shook me. I pulled away...I was crying. I thought he would at least be embarrassed and have some kind of sensible explanation for why he had this stuff...even if it was a lie that I could later pretend to believe...but Jason made me the "bad guy" for violating his trust. He screamed at me about the importance of trust in a marriage, which now, so many years later, seems rather laughable...however none of it was funny then.

I stood my ground. I told him he had to make a choice. It was either Dalton, Morgan and me...or the magazines, videos and sex toys. Jason looked me in the eyes and I could see he had long ago already made his decision. "Sorry, Babe. This is all bigger than you know."

I screamed…I told him to pack his filthy smut and get out of the house. I didn't want our children to be around him or his "collection" one more day. Jason looked at me and smirked. Then calmly began repacking his stash…and moved them, box by box, into our bedroom. "I'm serious," I screamed. "Get out…you're leaving tonight."

"No," he said, "I am not," as he continued to pack his boxes. "If anyone is leaving tonight…it looks like it's going to be you." With that, he went into our bedroom and shut the door. I was stunned. I cried…but I had made my stand. I gathered my calm and went into our bedroom. Jason was loading a video. Neither of us spoke. I packed a simple bag, got the kids and left. Oh Dear God, I thought…I am now a single mom with two kids…out on my own. Where am I going to go?

GETTING ON WITH IT
CHAPTER TWENTY-TWO

I N WRITING A book, the words sometimes don't flow just quite right...and the best laid chapter plans don't always match up. It seemed to me that I was getting behind with writing this book. I wanted to write so much more in the way of explanation about my relationship with Jason, but I was running late to meet the younger me on the bench outside of Tiffany's at the mall. I had always dreamed of a shopping trip to Tiffany's when I was a teenage girl...and I thought the younger me might appreciate the selection of location.

"So, I assume we are not going shopping today," the younger me said, as she walked up and sat down. "I guess this is more of a fantasy reconnaissance mission," she laughed.

"Let's think of it as a window shopping head start for the future," I said, knowing in my heart that one day I would be back to this same store with the real love of my

JESUS GIRL - Doing Real Life!

life. The younger me smiled. She looked about sixteen years old and was becoming…if I do say so myself…a quite attractive young woman in that smart, self-confident way that can never really be conveyed by outer beauty alone.

"So…," she asked, "why such a big deal with the porn?"

Her question was quite direct…and asked with great confidence. I knew right then that the younger me had actually been reading the book as I wrote each day…and I sensed that she had become a bit of a fan. Her question deserved a grownup answer, so I thought for a moment.

"It's not the one event…it is acknowledging what that event represents within an established pattern. People make bad choices…and God forgives, if they ask Him. But if one keeps going down a bad path…with no effort or attempt to change…God has no basis to offer his forgiveness," I said.

She nodded. "So the porn stash was just the straw that broke the camels back, right?"

"Yes…but that's too simple. It was the whole ongoing combination of things…the drugs, the cheating, the lies. In my heart, I realize now I should have done two things very differently."

"Never hook up with Jason in the first place, right?" the younger me smiled.

I recognized my own grownup sense of humor by watching the younger me talk. I laughed. "Yes, probably," I said. "But even more importantly, I was living my life to please a man…but I lost track of pleasing God. I was so desperate for Jason's approval and affection that I was willing to steer away from my own internal guidance."

"By internal guidance, you mean God?" This was a serious question from the younger me.

"Yes, that would be my answer now…but, back then, I wasn't even thinking along those lines. I was so wrapped up in me and others that I did not really think about God. And that is the single biggest mistake people make."

"Second?" the younger me asked.

"I should have paid more attention to the danger signs… the red flags…to my gut instincts…to the specific moments where Jason was telling me, without words, that things were terribly wrong. Each one of those things…simply by themselves…should have been a signal for me to cash in on 'God's Gift of Goodbye.'

The younger me nodded, waiting for me to continue. "And those things are?"

"First in my mind is physical abuse. If a man hits you once…he will most likely hit you again. I don't care how sorry he is or how much he says 'it will never happen again.' It will, most likely, happen again. And each time it will get worse. If he hits you once…get away to a safe place and get help."

The younger me nodded. I could tell that she had heard this advice before…just as I had heard it before. And, just like most women hit by a man, I didn't pay attention and really believed the apologies.

"The second issue is lying. If you catch someone in one lie…there are almost always other lies you haven't caught. Little lies lead to big lies…and lies destroy relationships."

"What about cheating?" the younger me asked.

"Marriage is a sacred bond between a man and a woman. Each pledges to the other to be true and faithful. If either one steps outside of the marriage…it will have a deadly impact on you and the whole family."

"What do you do about it?" the younger me asked.

"Well…each situation is different…and both the husband and wife need to be on the same page to save the marriage. However, the bottom line is…get help. It all boils down to keeping focus…and fidelity… on the marital relationship and the family. If either one ever loses that focus or that fidelity…it destroys the family…and that is never good in God's eyes."

"Like Jason's pornography?" the younger me asked.

"Yes…or constantly going to work early or always coming home late…or hanging out with friends at a bar when things at home are going undone."

"So, what happened when you left Jason that night?" she asked.

I laughed. I was glad she was interested. "Well," I said. "Just keep reading." With that, our meeting on the bench in front of Tiffany's was over.

DISCIPLINED SPIRIT
CHAPTER TWENTY-THREE

THE NIGHT I drove away from my married home…with our two young kids in the car…I obviously wasn't thinking clearly. Where would I go? Where would we live? How would I get the kids to school? How was I going to support my new life as a single mom? I cried.. and at that moment I knew I needed to have a plan.

I turned the car around and went back to our home. Jason was in his comfy sweats and t-shirt…eating a bowl of cereal. "I knew you'd be back," he said, then walked into our bedroom and shut the door. I told the kids to go to their rooms and leave me and their dad alone for awhile. Both kids were a bit shell shocked.

For one of the very few times in my life, I wanted to hit someone…and debated whether the victim would be Jason for his betrayal, or me for being so blind and stupid. I walked into our bedroom. Jason was on the bed watching TV. "So?" he asked, with a bit of a smirk on his face. "What now? You know you'll never find anyone better than me."

"I'm leaving and I mean it this time," I said. I could tell he knew I really didn't have anywhere else to go.

"Sure," he said, with an obnoxious cockiness that was one of his worst trademarks. "Good luck. I'll believe it when I see it."

I grabbed my robe, a pillow and a blanket and went to the living room to sleep on the couch, but sleep did not come easy. For one thing, Jason kept the TV on loud...plus, I knew I was going to have to come up with a plan. My mind was rolling over and over...spinning in circles.

For the next three weeks, Jason and I were physically living in the same house...but in reality, living very separate lives. Which, in all honesty, wasn't much different than our lives had been for the past several years...except now it seemed as if Jason made a special effort to throw his "flings" in my face and there were no more lame attempts at trying to hide the pot.

I tried to talk with Jason about the possibility of marriage counseling. He wanted nothing to do with the idea. I tried to talk with him about why pornography is so damaging to the human spirit and so destructive to human relationships...but he only laughed. I tried to talk with him about his cheating...and his sex addiction...and he called me uptight.

I had ended my "dancing" career at the club a few years earlier and had been working at a variety of odd type jobs. Although selling jewelry cleaner, doing multi-level marketing home shows and working as a receptionist didn't pay as well, it was certainly better hours and much more wholesome. I began looking for an apartment...and found a condo fifteen minutes away from our married home. It was a great place, but it meant that the kids would have to change schools. Although I didn't have the money for a downpayment on my own, my mother and step-father came up with a loan to help me swing the deal.

Separation or divorce is really hard on kids...and it hit my son Dalton even harder than I expected. He hated the new school, he became defiant and he absolutely hated my guts. On the other hand, my daughter Morgan had always been a really tough little girl ever since she was a baby...and she and I powered through. I was starting to feel good about myself and our new life in our new home...and all considered, life was starting to look pretty good. I found a job selling high-end seafood to upscale restaurants and my old confidence was coming back. I wanted to get back out into the world...I wanted to get back into life...and I wanted to kick some butt!

JESUS IN MY HEART
CHAPTER TWENTY-FOUR

WHEN I WAS a dancer...I was in great shape. Not just because of the actual physical energy and skill required for that kind of work, but because being in shape was one of the requirements if a girl wanted to keep her job. And for many deep, dark, psychological reasons that I only now understand...I really needed to keep that job. As a fish saleswoman, however, staying in that kind of shape became a bit more problematic. This is when I decided to really get more serious with my Taekwondo.

The art of Taekwondo takes more mental focus, stamina and skill than most people realize. I had been involved with the art on and off for several years...and the focus and attention to detail required to master the skill had helped me through some of my earlier ups and downs...in very interesting ways. But now I wanted to be even more focused, and I was. I jumped in...I wanted to learn...and I was going to be the best. Within six months,

I had my green belt. Within ten months, I had earned my brown belt and was starting to help teach the class. Eventually I was a full fledged black belt. Not only was I getting into great shape…I was also meeting new people and making new friends.

By this point, Dalton had moved back in with Jason…which, in looking back, is what most thirteen-year-old boys would do. Although at the time it hurt me, I knew his yelling, defiance and anger would not get any better by staying with his father. My worst nightmares about the ugly influences in Jason's home played through my mind. There were just too many temptations for a young teenage boy and I was concerned. Morgan, at least to me at the time, seemed to be adjusting quite well.

One of my best new friends at the Taekwondo studio was my main instructor, Mrs. Pretter. She talked a great deal about the importance of God in her life and she became a mentor to me, even in areas away from the sport. She invited me to go with her to church one Sunday, and in getting around that church crowd, I flashed back to my days at Hillcrest Christian School.

It was at Hillcrest so many years ago that I first met that guy named Jesus.…and those were very good memories. Although I am sure he was around me…and all of us…even back in my dancing days, no one, including me, was paying any attention. This new way of doing things…the bonding, the community, the sharing of faith… felt like family…and I was feeling really good.

I was really enjoying my Taekwondo workouts, which

I wanted to complement by joining a gym. It was at that gym that I first saw Bryan on a sunny day. He was very tall, very muscular, very charming...and very hot. Our eyes met...and he smiled. Over the next several weeks...we would chat a bit. Getting into another relationship at this point in my life had not even been on the radar screen, but things moved very quickly in that direction. He had a great sense of humor, he seemed like a real gentleman and...best of all...he really paid attention to me. He was good...really good with his moves...and he knew exactly what he was doing.

As our conversations progressed...he shared with me that he had been married once before, that he was lonely in the single life and that he had a little boy named Gregory. As Bryan and I spent more time together, I got to know his son...and Morgan, Gregory, Bryan and I would do fun things together. I was happy and we were starting to feel like a family.

MY MESSAGE FOR ALL
CHAPTER TWENTY-FIVE

FRIENDS OF MINE told me that writing a book like this would take a great deal of courage. I had no idea just how right they were until I outlined the hard truths about my life…where I have been, how I made a living, my blind, stupid mistakes…even short-sighted selfishness and a little bit of greed. I had always thought of myself as being a good and decent person…which I am now. But to lay out in writing a life's timeline…my background as a stripper…a failed marriage…and my failures as a mom…put the idea in my mind to start editing the timeline, to sanitize and to cut things out.

At one point, I was worried that those who had followed me in my ministry might judge me poorly if they knew the shortcomings of my past. But I decided that if I was to write this book…there couldn't be any secrets. I know God knows me and He knows my past…and I know that God loves me. I also know that He has forgiven me…just as He will forgive you at the moment you ask.

Should I have done more to try and save my "marriage" to Jason? In retrospect, I think I did all I could do…but others can debate that point from now until forever. But if a man steps out with other women…either flesh and blood women or pretend fantasy women on dirty videos or greasy magazine pages…is this right? No…not in God's eyes.

We can all agree that physical rape is wrong…and goes against God. But verbal abuse…on an ongoing basis…can do more long term harm because that memory lives hidden deep within. This kind of abuse is not good in God's eyes…and we, as women, cannot allow it to happen to ourselves, to our daughters or to our neighbors. This is why I so firmly believe in what I have come to call 'God's Gift of Goodbye.' God wants us to be whole and to be safe. If we are not whole and if we are not safe…God wants us to seek His guidance.

Why did I dance half naked in front of strange men? I told myself then that I needed the money. However, I now realize that I wanted to prove to my father that I was worthy, that I was attractive, that I could control men, that I could have power and that I could have money. These were the seeds planted by my own father's verbal abuse…one by one…bit by bit…drop by drop…cutting the spirit of my soul. It is these "little" things we let ourselves and others place on us by not following God's lead and God's very clear message for how he wants us to live our lives. Had someone helped me better know God...and had I taken my own responsibility to listen to God's Good Word...then the evil words and the bad actions of others could not have done such harm.

Have you ever seen anyone abuse or humiliate a child? That single act goes against God...and it needs to stop. Have you seen people crying in the street? Or children hungry? Or an old person alone? God wants us to work through Him to help address these issues. Just as evil can attack us one little step at a time...so can God's Truth... bit by bit, drop by drop...in a very powerful, healing way.

These words flow easy for me now...because I fully and absolutely live my life with God's Good Guidance. With that guidance, I also learned to know Jesus...not just in my head...but also in my heart. However, that wasn't always the case. As I sit here at this moment to write more back story from those difficult days, I know now that I still had some very hard lessons to learn.

ANOTHER BAD CHOICE
CHAPTER TWENTY-SIX

J UST BEFORE I started to write this chapter, I had an email from the younger me asking about progress on the book. She wondered why I hadn't been in touch the previous week. I wrote back telling her that what I needed to say to her this past week, I really wanted to say in writing...so that I would have a chance to edit, cut or change...soften, really...just a bit about me from those days...about the her she would become.

"What did you cut out?" she asked in a return email. "I think I really have a right to know."

"I decided not to change anything," I wrote back.

"So...what happened with Bryan? It sounds as if things finally turned out good for us."

I didn't want to lose my first fan by giving away the story...so I just wrote back "Keep reading. I will see you next week."

Like all of God's creations, Bryan was a mixed bag. He was tall, he was handsome...and he was a bit of a jerk to other people, but, at least at first, never to me. He was a sharp dresser, his personal hygiene top notch and he wore great cologne. He was also, at least superficially, a good dad to his son...and made it a point to keep his son in his life.

I think the first little lie...the crack in Bryan's manipulative facade...was when I found out that he was five years younger than me. I had never imagined being with a younger man and, to my surprise, he was quite uptight about being with an older woman. He made me promise not to tell anyone ever, which even at the time, struck me as odd since the difference in our ages was just five years.

At this point in our relationship I was living in my condo...and Bryan was still living with his mother. The nights he spent with me were great...but I know now that he was incapable of fidelity, truth or love. Again, my ingrained need for acceptance made me blind to what should have been glaringly obvious...and most likely would have been obvious even to me at that point in my life had I saved sex for marriage.

I was at a point where I needed to define my own life...down to basics such as 'what am I going to do for a living?' Morgan was living with me at the condo and Dalton would visit every other weekend. I needed to support myself, support the kids, support our home...and, at least partially, support my time with Bryan.

In sitting down with the classic yellow legal pad to outline my options and where I wanted to go with my life…I knew I needed to do something other than the "make do" kind of job that I had been doing up until that point. Every job that I had done…other than dancing…barely paid enough to just squeak by. And…even I knew at that point I would never go back to dancing.

The sales job with the upscale seafood company was a disaster almost from the start. The workplace harassment directed by the manager to the workers would most likely in today's world have landed him in jail…especially the day he threatened the back room fish cutters with a baseball bat. I stepped in and stopped the worst of it…but I knew I could no longer be around his almost daily threats and intimidation…and I left.

I then went to work at a weight loss clinic, which on the surface looked great…but knowing what I know now about good health and nutrition, it was mostly an overpriced scam…that barely paid enough to keep up with the rent. My next stop was selling knick-nacks at multi-level marketing home parties.

In sitting alone to scribble on the yellow note pad, I wrote down a list of my personal qualities. I was into health, I was into helping people and more than anything I was determined and disciplined. I also wrote down what I wanted in my life. I wanted to spend maximum time with my kids, I wanted weekends off, I wanted plenty of time to workout and, most importantly of all, I wanted to explore the fastest degree leading to a real job with the best pay and most flexible hours.

I looked at being a cop and I looked at being a gym manager. Neither job struck me as where I wanted to see myself in the next ten years time. Being a cop was dangerous and meant odd hours. Managing a gym meant dealing with oversized egos…and would just be a headache. So, out of everything I looked at, becoming a physical therapist struck me as an excellent choice. A much better choice, it turned out, than letting Bryan move in with me and Morgan.

THE LOOKING GLASS
CHAPTER TWENTY-SEVEN

GOD GIVES EACH of us an amazing internal guidance system. It works all of the time...24/7, day in and day out. The challenge for us...as humans...is to finely tune our internal listening device, which, I now know, is always easier if we remain on God's True Path. The day Bryan moved his first stuff into my condo, I saw him looking at himself in the mirror. I could tell he was in love...with his smile, with his body and with his "charming" personality.

"You know," he said, turning to me as I walked into the room, "you're really not in my league. You're lucky to have me." I was stunned. He laughed and just shrugged off what any other person on the face of the earth would have taken as a really terrible insult and put-down. Internally I was devastated...and I flashed back to the same kind of really hurtful put-downs I'd heard from my father as a little girl. Bryan was in full alpha male mode...with no regard for me or my feelings. My mistake at that point was that I convinced myself that it was just his immaturity, insecurity and narcissism giving me the put-downs.

As the weeks slid into months, Bryan seemed to grow bored with me and bored with having my daughter Morgan around. He started to have early morning and late night "work" assignments, which, even then, struck me as odd. I could tell that Morgan didn't like him…which was a third red flag that I realize now deserved more attention…but I was determined to make this new relationship work. I knew…or at least I convinced myself…that Bryan just needed a bit more time to settle in.

Physical Therapy school was tough…but I was enjoying it. We managed to survive on food stamps, my under-the-table part-time jobs…and the money Bryan got from his mom. As difficult as Bryan could be at times, I really wanted his attention and affection. I was determined to make this relationship work and against all common sense, I really believed I was succeeding.

Bryan was great at manipulating people and situations…and I realize now, he was a master at manipulating me because he knew how much I wanted a real family. One of the tools he used was his young son who he kept in the loop with Morgan and me…mostly at birthday parties and family gatherings with him, his mom and his ex-wife Shawna, who, it turned out, I really liked.

Shawna and Bryan had divorced, but stayed close to co-parent their son. At one point, Shawna invited me to go with her to church, an invitation that Bryan insisted I not accept. A few months later, when Bryan was working double shifts on a Sunday, Shawna called again with a church invitation. It sounded like something intriguing to do, so I accepted. Surprisingly, I had a good time and enjoyed the positive message. I told Shawna that I would enjoy going with her again at any point that Bryan was stuck working Sunday doubles.

When Bryan found out that I had been going to church with his ex-wife…he was furious. He drew a very clear line. I either was going to be with him…or with God. And I made the wrong choice.

As summer turned to fall, I was wrapped up in school and wrapped up in wanting to make the relationship with Bryan work, but he made it very hard. He became increasingly secretive on the phone, with texts and online chats. He would yell at me for no reason…then want to be kind and gentle as a way of apology. My daughter Morgan, told me straight out that she despised him.

My sex life with Bryan had been really good at first…but then he seemed to lose interest. I suspected another woman had come into his life, which, in retrospect, was partially true…but the real truth, which would come out later, was that he was sleeping around with ex-girlfriends and a variety of strangers. He always denied my suspicions and suggested that I was just being paranoid. He would woo me with his eyes and his charm and…like the naive fly with a very pretty spider…I would be spun into his web. In that web…without God's Good Guidance…I had become a blind fool.

LEARNING DISCERNMENT
CHAPTER TWENTY-EIGHT

GOD GIVES LITTLE children a special gift of discernment. Unfortunately, that gift is often ignored by the grownups in their lives…because the grownups are trying so desperately to bend reality to their own mind's idea of what they think things should be. That wonderful gift of discernment is then all too often trained out of children so that they are forced, often subconsciously, to see the world through the eyes of their closest grownups.

I have come to believe that we are all born with an internal "homing" device…a gift of discernment… which I now call God's Good Guidance. In my relationship with Bryan I saw in my mind's eye how I wanted our life to look, so I turned on my blind eye so that I would only see the world in the way I thought that world needed to be seen. However, in retrospect, I realize now that my-nine-year old daughter was seeing a different picture…and that a picture of her mom being manipulated, lied to and played was not a pretty picture or good life's lesson for one so young.

When I left to meet with the younger me, I purposely arrived 30 minutes ahead of time so that I could mentally organize my thoughts. Some of those who read this book might think that my greatest falling from God was my younger days working as a stripper. Others might judge me for leaving a failed marriage. One or two might point to my breast enhancement surgery. In my mind now...with the wisdom, clarity and insight that comes with age...I think my greatest failing was allowing my own internal guidance to be shut off in dealing with Bryan's evil web. I should have seen the warning signs...I should have listened to my young daughter's concerns...I should have followed those red flag warnings, which I now know were signals from God. But I didn't. I wanted to give the younger me a precise and concise explanation of how and why I went so terribly wrong. An explanation that would have helped me avoid so much pain and hurt had a grownup in my life bothered to have had that conversation with me when I was young.

The meetings with the younger me...as I wrote this book...had become something that I really enjoyed and it had become a bit of a game for me to suggest a meeting spot that would bring back memories for me and would be recognizable to her. For this meeting, I chose a set of outdoor tables near the old Baskin-Robbins ice cream shop downtown where I would go with my dad when I was a little girl. As the younger me walked up, she recognized the setting instantly.

"Baskin-Robbins," she said. "This is pretty retro." I nodded. I noticed that the younger me was now almost grownup...maybe seventeen or so...and almost at the point of going out on her early grownup life.

"The Bryan thing is really hard to talk about," I said.

"Why?" she asked.

"Because I hold that single time as the one time when I so completely...and utterly...turned my back on God," I answered.

"You mean you stopped believing in God?" she asked.

"No, not that. By 'turned my back' I mean that I allowed myself to turn off my own internal guidance and my own discernment. I got off God's path. If that internal guidance had been on full force...none of the soul crushing would have happened."

"How can you be so sure?" the younger me asked.

"I can be absolutely sure since I would not have allowed myself to have crossed any lines."

"Like?" she asked.

"Like," I said, "no sex before marriage."

"That's going to be a tough one," the younger me said, a point I would have agreed with when I was younger.

"Sure," I explained. "Although ultimately easier than you might think...and a great way to separate those guys who really love you from those who just want your body part-time."

The younger me laughed...and we both knew we had been there.

"The second thing," I continued, "is never let anyone demean you in the way that I let the men in my life demean me."

"Like the sex trips with Jason and Bryan?" the younger me asked.

"Yes," I said, "but even more to the less obvious point...is the verbal abuse and intentional manipulation...which can grind a person down to the point of almost no return. Manipulation, verbal abuse, cheating...all go against God's Good Guidance and His plan for you. All of those things are evil, wrong and go against what God set in motion for you in your life."

"Cheating?" she asked.

"Yes," I said. "That is always a big sign that you are just being used and abused. If a relationship can't be committed...why have a relationship at all?"

"So, how did things end with Bryan?" the younger me asked. She seemed especially interested. "When you first mentioned him...he sounded like quite a guy."

"I honestly thought he was a great guy. However, I soon discovered he was really only good at spinning deceit in such a way that his victims didn't even notice, myself included."

"Do you think he was a sociopath?" the younger me asked.

"Probably," I answered, "but that doesn't excuse me for not being more aware...for not following God and for not paying more attention to that internal guidance…as God meant. That was and is my responsibility. I realize now that I can't transfer that to anyone else…no matter the other person's particular personality flaws or manipulations."

"Let me grab us a couple of ice cream cones," I said to the younger me. And I'll share with you just how much worse it got with Bryan." The younger me smiled.

As I walked into Baskin-Robbins, the younger me waited outside at the table. The inside of the franchise was very familiar…and, indeed, retro. Everything was exactly as I remembered from so many years ago, except the prices, which were almost double. I knew that the younger me always got two scoops of chocolate fudge…as did I. As I walked back towards the door of the shop, a small piece of ice cream from one of the scoops broke off and landed on my finger. It slowly started to melt, so I rushed to where the younger me and I had been sitting so that I could give her one of the cones, freeing up my hand to fish a napkin from my back pocket. However, when I got back to the outdoor table, the younger me was gone. A small 3 x 5 piece of note paper was sitting on the table…fluttering in the slight breeze…held down by a small rock. There was handwriting that I recognized.

"You are an amazing person. I am so proud of how I turned out." It was signed "from me to you." And…at that moment…with melted ice cream on one hand, I knew I would never see the younger me again.

LOOKING LIKE A FOOL
CHAPTER TWENTY-NINE

MORE THAN A month had passed since I saw the younger me. Although I knew I would never see her again...I felt as if I was letting her down by not sharing more with her about what went wrong with my relationship with Bryan, as I had promised to share when we met outside the Baskin Robbins that warm afternoon. However, I wasn't making any progress on the book. Day after day I would sit before a blank computer screen...and nothing would come. What Bryan put me through in those days were things that no other human should ever have to endure. But, how do I explain all of that to other people? In explaining what happened to me, I felt I would just make myself look stupid and pathetic. I got to the point of almost giving up on finishing the book, then I had a dream.

If I am to help others with my ministry, then I need to bear my soul. God already knows about my past life...what happened to me with Bryan...and all of my other shortcomings. I also know that He has forgiven me...just as He will forgive you at the exact moment you ask. My problem...what I was shown in the dream...was that I had not yet fully forgiven myself for being exactly what I feared others would think. I was, indeed, a sad, stupid and pathetic loser...and there was some block within me that was holding me back from sharing that part of the story.

In the dream...which had me sitting at a table...I was presented with a question on a piece of white paper. How could I help others find their own forgiveness through a living relationship with Jesus Christ...if I couldn't even forgive myself? Personal ego was my block. I didn't want to look bad in the eyes of others...and that was shameful. It was also unnecessary since I had long ago already been forgiven, and...like a flash...my fingers began to race across the keyboard.

Bryan was hot. I wrote that in an earlier chapter. I was attracted to him physically and I wanted so very desperately for him to like me... then to love me. I wanted his acceptance and his approval...and I jumped into the sexual phase of our relationship with no thought or discussion whatsoever about marriage or monogamy. Bryan told me more than once that I was not...from a beautiful body and intellectual standpoint...in his league and that I needed to know that I was one lucky woman to have him. I was so blind at that point that I felt lucky...and I believed him. And...that's very sad.

I suspected he was sleeping with other women…but I convinced myself that I was just being overly jealous. Bryan said he wanted me more blonde…so I became blonder. He liked trendy dressers…so he started, literally, dressing me in his favorite trendy styles from his own favorite trendy store. He twisted my mind to a point where my own personality and self-esteem was totally gone… while all the time I was so blind that I honestly believed that I was doing the right thing to build a new "family" and to earn the approval of my man.

In looking back, Bryan was most certainly a sociopath. He was brilliant at manipulating people and events…and doing it in such a way that everyone in his circle, including me, was seduced ever so subtly into his web. My children's father, Jason, was as he was…not very ambitious, not very bright, what some might call a born loser. However, Bryan was truly an evil person…and I was so blind and naive that I did not see it until I was captured.

Bryan put pressure on me to bring other women into our bed. I told him that I had no interest in that…but he kept insisting. I adamantly refused, but he made me feel guilty for not being a "good lover" and more understanding of his special needs. He would sometimes pull my hair and force me onto the floor…all the while looking at himself in the mirror. If I didn't pretend to play along…he would tell me that he lost interest in me…and would virtually deny my existence for days at a time while he disappeared into our bedroom for private online chats and secret texting.

The sad circle...the one that traps so many young girls and women...was the circle Bryan created for me and which I allowed myself to be placed. The more he rejected me and my emotional needs, the more I felt I needed to be "better" to save our relationship, to save our new "family" and to keep his "love" and affection. He knew how to play people...and he played me quite well.

As I write this story...intentionally leaving out the more degrading aspects of Bryan's verbal abuse and what he forced me to do...I do not want to put the blame for my failures on him or on any one else. Yes...I failed at my marriage to Jason and now I was "failing" at my relationship with Bryan. It would be so easy to try and put the blame on them, but I know now that the blame needs to be put squarely on me. Not because I was a bad person...and not because I did not try. I failed because I became blind to what was going on around me and I had disregarded everything that I now know God wants from us if we are to live a Good Godly Life. Yes, my earlier fears as I tried to write this chapter were correct. I was a pathetic loser, but God had not created me to be a loser. I made myself that way by letting myself...bit by bit, inch by inch...turn my back on God. That was squarely, 100% my failure to own.

UP FROM THE BASEMENT
CHAPTER THIRTY

As the emotional, verbal and mental abuse from Bryan deepened in our private lives behind closed doors, he continued to charm almost everyone around him. He was Bryan…he was super handsome…and he could do no wrong. He was strutting through life, manipulating everyone and everything…and getting a sick and twisted jolt out of pushing me lower and lower to service his needs. I felt trapped and saw no way out. Although I did not recognize it at the time, I had let myself become so completely separated from God that I had lost control of my own self, my own being and my own soul. I was allowing another person to denigrate and degrade me for the benefit of his own inflated ego. I let it happen…and the more I tried to go along…the worse it became. The more I tried to be "good" by Bryan's standards…the worse he treated me. I was depressed and felt as if Bryan was trying to push me out of my mind and out of my soul.

As I write the above paragraph, I know now that we can eliminate evil from our lives by being on a right path with God. Even if we stray…as I strayed then…we can always find that path because God has lit it so brilliantly. It is not always an easy path to follow…but it is a simple one…and on that brilliant path we will always find forgiveness, redemption and a way out…if we just ask. But I knew none of that the late night I sat on my bed with the fifth of vodka, a razor blade and two dozen Seconals.

As I looked at the tools for my own destruction aligned on the nightstand, I knew that my daughter would be better off without me…because I was such a failure. My son would be better without me, too…he didn't really like me anyway. I had no money, I had no job…and I had nowhere to go. All I knew…as I forced that first shot of vodka past my tonsils…was that I could not face Bryan again. I could not face what he forced me to do. I could not face the abuse. I could not face my kids, I could not face my mom…but, worst of all, I could not face myself. From my perspective, that desperate night, everyone and everything would be so much better if I was just gone.

I cried and I prayed. I looked at the bottle of pills. I cried some more…I prayed some more…and then I really started to pray…in the old fashioned hard knee kind of way. I prayed more intensively and deeply than I had ever prayed before. I hate the taste of vodka, I don't like pills…and I certainly wasn't into cutting. "Dear

God," I prayed. "Please give me some sort of a sign." And, at that exact moment, I felt God's peace come upon me.

From out of nowhere, I thought of Shawna...who I hadn't seen in weeks and who I was sure knew nothing about my desperate situation. At any other time in my life I would never have dreamed of calling my current boyfriend's ex-wife...but Shawna's face came to my mind as I prayed...so I picked up the phone, I reached out to Shawna and even at 1:00am, she answered.

When she came on the line, she said she could tell that I had been crying. With that permission to cry, the floodgates opened...and I cried even louder and more deeply. I shared things with her that I had never shared with anyone before. I told her that Bryan was a liar and a cheat...a really brilliant manipulator of people...and a not so closeted narcissist. I told her that he used people in very ugly ways. I told her the specifics of the sexual degradation. I told her about the humiliation and mind manipulation. She could have hung up at any time...but she let me talk.. she let me vent. That night...for more than three hours...way into the wee hours...as Shawna listened to me cry and tell my story, she helped me develop a plan and I began to see a way out of my un-Godly trap.

THE ART OF SELF-PARENTING
CHAPTER THIRTY-ONE

O F ALL THE people in the world…Shawna had lived what I had been living…and she had been smart enough to get away from Bryan. She had survived. She was encouraging. She gave me honest, straightforward, Godly advice. She talked me through the most desperate night of my life. She helped me see I was not crazy and that God had a meaning and a purpose for my life. She helped me focus on the real issue I was facing. If life with Bryan was unbearable, Shawna told me…then, I needed to leave. I knew in my heart that Bryan was really, really sick…in a dangerous and twisted way. And I knew at that moment…by talking with Shawna…that God would give me the courage to leave.

As I hung up with Shawna, the plan that emerged was that Morgan and I would move out that next morning. We would pack a few things…and just leave. Since I had no money and nowhere to go, I would move into the basement at Shawna's parents' home in the far suburbs. I would at least have a roof over my head and a safe place for me and Morgan to stay while I finished PT school, got a job and could start earning my own living.

Dave and Debbie, Shawna's parents, were the definition of God's Mercy, God's Grace…and God's Unconditional Love for a stranger. They didn't talk big and they didn't make a show of giving. They had comfortable lives, they were thankful for the gifts they had been given…and they knew when a return gift was good to give. With no quizzing nor questions asked…Morgan and I became family.

Dave and Debbie had a large split-level house which had been Shawna's childhood home before she went out to make a life on her own. On the lower level was a large finished basement with what most people would call a family room. There was also a bathroom and two very nice small bedrooms. I found out later that Dave and Debbie had offered this type of Godly refuge to many others over the years…others facing a transitional crisis and needing a short-term helping hand. My daughter Morgan shared with me that she had become frightened around Bryan…so she saw our new digs in the basement at Dave and Debbie's as a real step up.

As I think back it strikes me as odd to the point of almost humorous that I would move into my ex-boyfriends's ex-wife's parents' home…into a basement that Dave and Debbie themselves called the Heart Break Hotel. At the time it was a real blessing and a wonderful lifeline. I had no real job skills, no savings, nowhere to turn. I was broke. Who does that? The ex-boyfriend's ex-wife's parents? These people were truly amazing...close to God and dedicated to His work.

As my bad financial situation became obvious, Dave and Debbie graciously offered me some part-time work cleaning the bathrooms at their business office. That led to some other jobs like...grocery shopping, cooking and painting...anything I could do to help me and Morgan get through to my PT graduation. The rules in Dave and Debbie's home were very simple, but strict. Keep the place clean, be home at night and no boyfriend visitors. Dear God...it felt good to be home...and to be truly loved by others.

As my first few weeks of settling in at Dave and Debbie's turned into three months...then six months...then a year...I had a chance to see a real Christian home in action. It wasn't about dressing up and going to church on Sundays, although we did just that. But for me it was more about what happened the rest of the week. They listened to me and my worries...hour after hour. They loved me when I felt unloveable. They never judged me...even when I was judging myself negatively. They not only talked the talk, but they walked the Godly walk. Walking again with Jesus not only became a big part of my new life....it became the biggest part of my life and put me on the road to my greatest calling. I was free, I was happy and I could breath again.

I realized how patterns we are shown as young children can have a very negative impact on decisions we make as adults. In talking with the younger me, I realized that I was actually giving myself the good advice that my parents would have given me if they would have been more aware. I also realized that this was a practice run for advice I would give my own daughter and, now, for others to give their daughters, their grand daughters and their fellow daughters in Christ, no matter the blood relation.

Being in Dave and Debbie's basement…like a daughter in their home…I learned how a Christian family works and how living on God's Brilliant Path takes away the concern and confusion wrought by others. I began to understand the bad choices I had made in the past…and I was able to see the problems I caused for myself, my children and our well-being. Problems caused because I had turned my back on God, His Commandments and His plan for me. I took full responsibility…and I saw how to fix things.

STRIPPER TO PREACHER
CHAPTER THIRTY-TWO

HAD GIVEN MY presentation in Tulsa, OK one very cold and windy January afternoon. After I had finished speaking, a line of ladies formed, as seems to almost always happen…to either thank me for what I had to say or to share insights from their own lives. More than once, women have told me that my presentation gave them permission to speak about things that they had never shared with anyone. I would hear stories of infidelity, betrayal, hard times, disobedient children, inattentive husbands, sexual abuse, past bad choices and, most often, the pressure that these women felt they were under to live up to other people's expectations. The expectations that they had themselves…over the years…allowed others to place on them.

This particular day, one woman waited at the very end of the line, letting everyone else go ahead of her so that she would be the last to greet me. She shook my hand firmly...then told me quite forcefully that she could in no way relate to any part of my story whatsoever. She came from a wonderful family, her father adored her, she had never had the desire to be a stripper, she didn't go to bars, she didn't drink alcohol, her husband had never strayed, no one in her home ever looked at pornography, her children were all happily married and she had never been divorced.

"Well, praise God," I said. I had the impression that she was looking for a fight.

"Praise God, yes," she said. "But why do you feel that you are so much better than the rest of us and have to parade yourself up there on stage, as if your life is such a wonderful example?"

Now I knew she was looking for a fight. "First of all," I said, as calmly as one can say when surprised in this way, "I hold my life up not as an example of how others should live...but as an example of how each of us can stray from God's Good Path without consciously knowing that we are straying."

"So when you were a stripper...you thought you were doing God's work?" She asked, coming across as a very rude cable news reporter, looking for some sort of salacious, trumped up scandal.

"When I was stripping...God wasn't part of the equation...and that is really the core essence of my message. If we turn our back on God, then we allow things into our lives that are destructive and lead in directions that are away from God's plan for us."

"Well, I still feel as if I wasted my time and the cost of lunch to be here. You and your life offer nothing that I can relate to."

"Then you are very fortunate to have avoided the hurts that sting so many others, " I told her. "But… what about my story of the husband and wife who took me into their basement…shared their home…and offered a real sense of family at my most desperate time? They had good lives, they had a beautiful home, they had a happy marriage…and they were fortunate enough to avoid the really bad pitfalls that hit so many others. In my heart, they were the very essence of God's Grace and God's Mercy. Maybe you can relate to that part of my story?"

"That's ridiculous," she said. "I would never let a stranger move into my basement."

With that, I shook the woman's hand, wished her the best, offered my blessings… and told here that I needed to pack my things for my drive back home that night. I wished her well and have, from time to time, wondered if she ever fully understood what I said about God's Mercy. If her life was as good as she shared, then I prayed that she would find it in her heart to share her good fortune with others less fortunate.

As I moved closer to finishing this book, I wanted to end it with fireworks to celebrate God's Good Love for all of us. I wanted to see the sky filled with bright and colorful lights and joyous explosions to celebrate His greatness and the impact that He can have on all of us…once we invite him in. But the more I thought about fireworks, the more silly the notion seemed, because God works His wonders quietly, steadily, 24/7, without stop...but only if we invite Him into our lives.

God also forgives. Not in some mysterious way...not by waiting in line...not with the help of a paid consultant...and certainly not on a deferred monthly installment plan. God's forgiveness is exact, specific and immediate...once we ask for that forgiveness.

Living a good Godly Life is not always easy...especially with the pressures of modern life, modern temptations and the expectations that others place on us. But living that kind of life is simple, very simple. God knows your hurt, God knows your pain, God knows all of the things you did...and all of the things that you should have done, but didn't. Do you want to get on God's path? Simple...just ask, with no regard to those people or things that want to pull you off that path.

That afternoon at the airport in Phoenix, when I found out from my doctor that I had cervical cancer, sticks in my mind with laser-like focus. I had just finished my studies to become a minister. I had fallen in love more than I had ever fallen in love before...and all of the hurt and struggle was, I thought, behind me.

As I boarded the plane for LAX, I was in a daze. I called the most important person in my life, my husband Joe. On that terrible night...we had already been married for three years and had been through a great deal together. Joe told me we would get through this, too…that God would guide…and said he would catch the next flight out to LA.

My life had been so filled with failures and failed relationships that I had questioned if I would ever get married again. I had Jesus Christ in my life…and that was my greatest blessing. If God had a mate planned for me, then I was willing to wait. And if I was going to wait…it would need to be a Godly Marriage, special for me and revealed by God.

When a mutual friend first introduced us, I told Joe straight out that I had zero interest in "dating" if his definition of dating was sex. Unlike so many other guys…Joe actually felt that same way. I didn't need my personal validation from a man, and Joe certainly did not need his validation from me. I liked him…and he liked me. As God intended…that "like" turned into a once in a lifetime, glowing, perfect Godly Match. My love for him and his love for me was the deep foundation, the real deal.

As I thought of Joe, I started to cry. I flashed back to Lido Key…on that beautiful white sand beach…as the sun set… when Joe asked me to be his wife. I could tell that he loved me so much. How could I live without him? How could he live without me? Against all odds, we now had each other, but that was going to be taken away by disease and death. When the plane landed in LA, I took a cab to my room and completely collapsed into tears.

I felt so alone. I fell to my knees…and I prayed. "Dear God," I asked, "I have been through so much, I have worked so hard, I have a gift to give...and my life is going really well. Why me? Why now?"

With that prayer...at that moment...a most wonderful and amazing calm came over my spirit and my entire body. And God answered back. "Who better than you and when better than now?" With that...I had my answer. I would finish my studies and be credentialed. I would found a ministry and travel the nations to teach others how to share their courage, God's Good Word and God's Good Lessons with those around them. I would encourage other women to speak to their daughters, their grand-daughters and their neighbors who are willing to listen. I would love Joe as he and I both needed to be loved, and...I would beat the beast called cancer.

When Joe arrived that next morning, he was more distraught than me...and I think he was surprised that I was both calm and alert. We hugged and he held me. It felt good to be in his strong arms. I promised him...as I had promised God the night before...that I would beat the odds and beat the cancer.

My doctor told me that I had just a year to live, but God told me not to believe the doctor. My doctor had a list of things for me to do, but, with prayer, I saw those things as mostly poisonous and ineffective. Luke 1:37 came to my mind - "Nothing is impossible with God." From that point on, doors opened and miracles happened. Organic foods, natural healing, prayer...stay away from medical poison...and build your own immune system as God intended.

Joe had always been a believer in Jesus Christ...at least later in his life. Now he was a believer in natural health and natural healing as he watched me lead the way and set the example. My mainstream medical doc was amazed, as was everyone around me. The more I took charge of my own health...with God's Good Guidance...the more I felt empowered to share my message with others. I was healed...physically, emotionally and spiritually. And I wanted to tell the world!

Am I a perfect person? No...I definitely have bad days. Have I always led a perfect life? If you've read this far...you know that I have not. Do I live my life with God at the center of everything? Yes, now I do. Have I been forgiven for past mistakes? Yes. Will I make mistakes in the future? Most likely. But with God's Good Guidance, all of us can minimize the negative impact of bad things in our lives...and we can help others do the same in their own lives. We can offer God's Mercy, God's Grace...and God's Unconditional Love for a stranger when times are good for us. With prayer, we will receive the same at exactly the time that we need it most.

As I prayed alone that night...in the dark, in my room in Los Angeles, with the false knowledge that I was going to die with cancer...I was more focused and direct with prayer than I had ever been in my life. Those prayers were answered with "words" from God and an etched roadmap of not only what I should do and where I should go...but also with directions of how to help myself and millions of others get there.

I must admit here that I had never been completely comfortable in my own skin, but with God's etched roadmap that night, I was at peace. God created me in his image…just as he created you in His image…and that image is perfect, imperfections and all. If we trust in God…God will make it Right.

In one blinding flash, God showed me the tools and approach I would need to cure my cancer…and with prayer and a lot of hard work…the cancer was cured. God showed me that I would continue my studies, be credentialed and travel to bear witness to many others…and I have. God showed me the way to a real, Godly Marriage…and I found that with Joe. God showed me how to heal myself from the inside out…and how to help my children heal their own lives. Both kids are doing quite well…and both have discovered a renewed faith and purpose in life through Jesus Christ. Against all odds…God showed me that I should set aside a year of my life to write a book…a book that told about my journey, my many failings, the hard knock lessons that I learned and how those lessons could help others. And this, my dear friends, is the book that I wrote.

EPILOGUE

A LMOST A YEAR and a half has passed since I began the process of writing this book. In many ways it seems as if time has zipped by with amazing speed. On some days it has seemed as if I've lived through half a lifetime. I have learned so much about myself, those around me and the choices...both good and bad...that people make. This process has given me insights and taught me lessons that I might not have learned had I not decided to make this journey. As I sat some days staring at a blank computer screen, memories would come flooding in...not all good...some quite painful...but all important in helping me put this story into perspective. And with that perspective I was able to see quite clearly where and how I got off God's Good Path and how I was able...with the help of others...to once again find my way.

During the past eighteen months...I found three new grey hairs, two new smile lines and added an extra pound or two. But after my very scary brush with cancer,

I consider all of these little signs of life as a blessing from God. Also during this time I was forced to have some pretty grownup conversations with my now grown children. I knew they would eventually read this book…and that some of their friends and the parents of their friends would read this true story of me, my life and my irresponsible actions that, for a time, could not help but impact their lives in a way that was counter to God's plan for their lives. At first those conversations were very awkward for each of us…yet, it turns out, those conversations strengthened our bond and let me begin to know my own "children" as the wonderful adults they have become.

As life moves on…sometimes like the tick of a slow clock and sometimes like a speeding bullet…I continue to fall more and more in love with my husband Joe. Our love is the real, deep, faithful and faith-based eternal love that burns like the hottest steel foundry. The kind of burning love that one can only experience in a good, Godly marriage. And…like any foundry fire…that flame needs to be stoked and nurtured each and every day. By me…and by Joe. Our life together works because we both work hard at our marriage…and because our marriage and our lives are guided by God.

In writing this book I must admit that there were times that I cried. I cried because I was so very sad remembering some of the things that I allowed myself to do. I cried because I could not believe the stupid ways I turned my back on God and God's plan for me. But even more often, I cried with joy at happy memories and in gratitude for those who surrounded me when I most needed guidance, support and good life lessons. I thank you for reading this book...and I pray, Dear God, that this book has allowed me to share important lessons with you...so that you, in turn, can share those lessons with the people in your life who are most important to you.

"I will bless you...and so you shall be a blessing.
  And in you...
    all families and peoples of the Earth will be blessed."
                  -Genesis (12:2,3)
                  (paraphrased)

ALTAR CALL

I HAVE TRAVELED ALL across our great nation…and have spoken to thousands of people, from all walks of life. Although we all seem so different, one from the other…almost everyone strives for the same basic necessities, the same basic human dignity and the same sense of purpose in our lives.

For me, I found my purpose by having a living relationship with Jesus Christ. That relationship is the bedrock foundation of everything that is good…and has allowed me to see God's Promise and God's Purpose for my life. Would you like to give your life to Jesus? Would you like to completely and absolutely invite the living Christ into your heart? If you have never asked Jesus into your heart before…then there is no better day than today. And there is no better time than now. All you have to do is turn to the next page in this book and read the very simple prayer out loud:

"Lord Jesus...I confess with my mouth...

and believe in my heart...

that you died on a cross and that you rose again.

I ask that you forgive me of all my sins...

Thank you that you love me.

In Jesus Name...Amen!"

And with that simple prayer my dear sister or brother in Christ...you are now part of the family of God!

Andrea Thompson
Moving Beyond Ministries
LifeCall@MovingBeyondMinistries.com

"*Everyone who calls on my name will be saved!*"

-Jesus of Nazareth
(Romans 10:13)

ABOUT THE AUTHOR

Andrea Thompson is the Founder of Moving Beyond Ministries. She travels extensively talking with other Christian Ministries, Christian outreach groups, youth groups and civic organizations. Her next book in this series deals with natural food, natural healing and how she beat terminal cancer. For more information about Andrea Thompson and the mission statement of Moving Beyond Ministries, go to MovingBeyondMinistries.com.

BOOKING ANDREA THOMPSON
GUEST SPEAKER

Andrea Thompson is considered by many to be one of this generation's most dynamic Christian motivational speakers. Thompson has appeared before church congregations, women's ministries and youth groups nationwide. For booking information, go to MovingBeyondMinistries.com.

BULK QUANTITY BOOK SALES
SPECIAL DISCOUNT PRICING

"Jesus Girl - Doing Real Life" is available at special discount prices direct from the publisher. This book can be a wonderful adjunct for age appropriate junior high level life education, young women's Christian study groups or as a tool for church or group fundraising efforts. Special First Edition autographed copies are available on request. For For Bulk Sales Contact:
MOVING BEYOND MINISTRIES
816-292-2846
Email us at: Info@MovingBeyondMinistries.Com

CPSIA information can be obtained at www.ICGtesting.com
Printed in the USA
LVOW04s2313120215

426819LV00001B/1/P